Why do puppies chew slippers?

When Mickey Wonders Why, he searches out
the answers with a little
help from these friendly experts:

Vice President and Publisher Cathryn Clark Girard
Director, Product Development Kristina Jorgensen
Editorial Director Lisa Ann Marsoli

DK Direct Limited

Managing Art Editor Eljay Crompton
Senior Editor Rosemary McCormick
Writer Alexandra Parsons
Illustrators The Alvin White Studios and Richard Manning
Designers Wayne Blades, Veneta Bullen, Richard Clemson,
Sarah Goodwin, Diane Klein, Sonia Whillock

©1992 The Walt Disney Company
No portion of this book may be reproduced
without the written consent of The Walt Disney Company.
Printed in the United States of America
ISBN:1-56326-210-X

Contents

Why do cats always land on their feet?

Because, as a cat falls through the air it twists its body around so it always lands on outstretched legs. This is a reflex action, which means the cat doesn't have to think about it, its body just does it. It's like sneezing. You don't have to think about it, you just do it!

Cat nap
What happened to the cat who swallowed a ball of wool?
She had mittens!

Bald kitty!
Here's a cat without fur. It's called a sphynx. Even though it doesn't have fur, it still feels warm and soft.

Going for a swim
There are lots of different kinds of pet cats, and most of them HATE water. But here's one that doesn't. The Turkish swimming cat likes taking a dip.

Purr-fect cat care

☞ Cats sleep anywhere. They spend a lot of the day curled up snoozing or resting. At nighttime they like to go out and play.

☞ Cats like to be cuddled and stroked but, like people, sometimes they want to be left alone.

☞ Cats like to eat fish and meat.

5

Why do puppies chew slippers?

Because they've got to chew something!

As their teeth start to come through, their jaws itch and ache. Chewing on something helps the pain go away and makes them feel better.

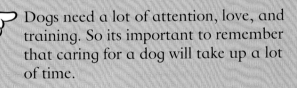

Good dog!
A dog that is well cared for makes a happy and loyal companion. Some dogs can be trained to help people with disabilities get around.

It's a dog's life!

 Dogs like to go for walks every day.

Grown-up dogs can eat two meals a day. They enjoy meat and dog biscuits.

Dogs need a lot of attention, love, and training. So its important to remember that caring for a dog will take up a lot of time.

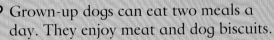

Wild dog!

There are dogs that live in the wild. The Australian dingo roams around the countryside, hunting sheep and chickens, which makes farmers very angry. And – it doesn't bark!

Noisy friend
Which pet is the loudest?
A trum-pet!

Is a guinea pig really a pig?

No, it's a rodent – other members of the rodent family are mice and hamsters. It's called a pig because it trots like a pig, rather than scurries along like a mouse. It is also shaped like a small pig.

Wild pigs
Guinea pigs come from the warm grasslands of Brazil and Peru, where they live in large groups called colonies. They were originally raised to be eaten, just like chickens.

All dressed up
In Europe, guinea pigs are popular pets. There are even special shows for them. Owners curl their pets' fur to make them beautiful for the judges.

Guinea pig hints

☞ Guinea pigs like to have guinea pig friends.

☞ They eat dried grass such as hay and they chew on hard things to wear down their growing teeth.

☞ In warm weather pet guinea pigs can live in outdoor cages.

Do mice like cheese?

They do, but they're not crazy about it. Mice eat cheese, soap, and candle wax because they like the fat in them. They also like starch, and will eat wallpaper because the glue on the back contains lots of it. But most of all, mice like to eat seeds, like corn or wheat.

Mouse nest

When baby mice are born they are blind and deaf and completely bald. But their mothers think they're cute!

Mouse manners

Mice sit up on their back legs to eat, holding the food in their paws. As they nibble they spit out the bits they don't like.

Pet mice

 Just like hamsters, pet mice like to have a cage with a wheel in it so they can run around.

 Mice like to sleep a lot of the time.

Mice use their claws for grooming and scratching.

Do horses sleep standing up?

They do and they don't. Horses take five or six hour-long naps a day. They take most of them standing up, and one or two lying down. Horses don't sleep all night because a long time ago when most horses were wild, they had to be on the lookout for animals who might attack them.

Small fry
The smallest horses in the world are the Falabella horses of Argentina. They are usually 30 inches tall and weigh around 100 pounds. That's as big as a large dog!

Horseshoes
Horses that don't live in the wild, wear horseshoes for the same reason people wear shoes – to protect their feet when they walk on hard surfaces.

Happy horses

👉 Did you know that the horse and the rhinoceros come from the same animal group?

👉 They're happy munching on things like grass, hay, oats, and barley.

👉 Horses like a lot of exercise. They like company, too!

13

Why do rabbits wiggle their noses?

Because they are constantly sniffing the air. Rabbits have very sensitive noses and a strong sense of smell. Their sense of smell tells them if danger is close by. Smell is also the main way rabbits communicate with each other. Sniff, sniff!

Cottontail

Cottontail rabbits are wild rabbits. They have short, bushy tails with a white underside that can easily be seen from a distance. That's how they keep an eye on one another. At the first sign of danger, if one rabbit hops to it, they all hop to it!

Bunny facts

☞ It's best to keep pet rabbits in a snug, dry house called a hutch, with nice clean hay to sleep on.

☞ They enjoy munching on corn, oats, carrots, and fresh green vegetables.

How big do turtles get?

There are different kinds of turtles in all different sizes. They can be just three inches long, or as big as six feet long. The largest turtle is called the leatherback, and it can weigh as much as 1,500 pounds. This is NOT the kind of turtle you want for a pet!

16

Big fella

This is the largest tortoise in the world. It is called the Aldabran giant tortoise. Tortoises are a kind of turtle that will only live on land. Tortoises are becoming quite rare. So many people think it's best not to keep them as pets.

Bony back

The South American green turtle lives in the wild. It has a shell made of 60 bony plates which cover its back and stomach.

17

Turtle time

☞ A turtle's shell is its home.

☞ Turtles like to eat plants and insects.

☞ Tortoises sleep all through the winter.

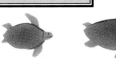

Why do hamsters stay up all night?

Because hamsters are nocturnal (nock-TUR-nal) creatures, which means they stay up all night, and sleep all day. Some hamsters are nocturnal because their natural home is a very hot desert. In the desert it's too hot to move during the day, but it gets nice and cool when the sun goes down.

Cheeky pouches

Hamsters store food in special pouches in their chubby little cheeks. Then they scurry off and hide the food, so they can eat it later.

Happy hamsters

☞ Hamsters are clean, quiet, cute and they like to be cuddled.

☞ They enjoy climbing, exploring, and playing.

☞ Hamsters will sometimes move the contents of their cage around.

Marathon hamster

Hamsters need a lot of exercise. It's best if they have a running wheel in their cage. They will run between four and eight miles on their wheels every night!

Why do parrots talk?

Because they like the sound of their own voices! Parrots will copy the sounds they hear in the house, such as the sound of the telephone ringing and the way people talk or sing. But they're not actually talking, just copying sounds.

Pretty polly?
Baby parrots look pretty weird. But by the time they're ready to leave Mom they've grown to be big and beautiful.

Top talkers
Some parrots are better at copying human sounds than others. African gray parrots are the best talkers. They are friendly birds, but only to people they know well.

Parrot facts

 Parrots like their owner to give them a shower once a week.

 They like to have toys to play with.

They like to eat birdseed, fruit, and nuts.

Do goldfish get bored?

Scientists don't think so, even though you'd imagine they would, swimming around and around the same old bowl or fish tank every day. But goldfish don't get bored because they have terrible memories! They can't remember anything that happened more than 15 seconds before.

Growing up gold
Baby goldfish are often born a dull greenish-black color. They turn gold as they grow up.

Try keeping this in a tank!
Goldfish are members of the carp family. Some carp can grow to be about three feet long.

Hello, hello
What's the best way to communicate with a fish?
Drop it a line!

Keeping goldfish happy

Pet goldfish like to be in big tanks with gravel on the bottom and plenty of plants and rocks to hide under.

23

Do all canaries sing the same song?

No, they don't. Different kinds of canaries have their own way of singing and their own kinds of songs. Birds learn songs from their parents and it may take quite a while for the young birds to get to know all the different ways to put the notes together.

Music lessons
The best singers in the canary family are roller canaries. They sing so beautifully, they are used to "teach" other canaries how to sing.

A boat full of songs
Canaries originally came from the Canary Islands. Over 350 years ago, a boat carrying singing canaries sank in the Mediterranean sea. The birds escaped and settled on other islands.

Tweet, tweet
Which bird can lift the
heaviest weight?
The crane!

25

Canary habits

☞ Canaries like lots of water
for drinking and bathing.

☞ They like to eat birdseed,
soft leaves, and buds.

☞ It's best to keep a pet
canary in a big, clean
cage.

Do all animals make good pets?

No, they don't. Some animals just shouldn't be pets because they wouldn't be happy away from their natural home. But there are some animals that, with a lot of care, might fit into your home quite nicely – even though they're a little unusual.

Move over

Imagine having a pot-bellied pig or a chinchilla sitting on your couch. Some people train these animals to live in their homes and become part of the family.

Hi, pal!

Goats can be kept in backyards. As long as they have food and shelter, they'll be happy. They'll even provide milk.

Pets, and more pets

Pets give us comfort and affection. In return they need to be loved, fed, and cared for. If you have a pet, or you would like to have one, it's important to remember that they need your time and special care.

Take care

Salamanders are amphibians (am-PHIB-ee-ans). They are tricky pets though because you should NEVER pick them up.

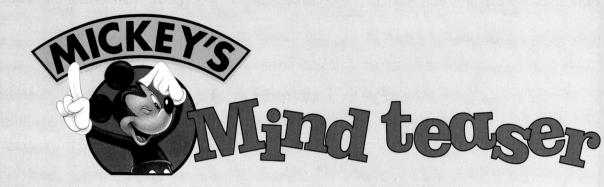

MICKEY'S Mind teaser

Animals like to stay in their own special places. Can you match each animal with its own cozy place.